Hamlet II
King of Denmark

A Play in Five Acts

David A. Lariscy

Eximius Books

Eximius Books

Published in 2012 by **Eximius Books**. Eximius Books is a publisher of unique books in the Literature and Fiction category. You can find more information on **Eximius Books** on the web at::

www.EximiusBooks.com.

Cover art provided courtesy of Beautiful Events, found on the web at: www.BeautifulEvents.org.

Library of Congress Control Number (LCCN): 2012933808

ISBN-10: 0985289902
ISBN-13: 978-0-9852899-0-4

Acknowledgments

This play was published on the occasion of my 80th birthday. The following dedications are from my family:

- *From your wife —I love you and am very proud of your accomplishment with this play.*
- *From your son — Your passion for reading and writing inspired me to do the same. I love you Dad!*
- *From your daughter - By the way you lived your life, I learned to love God, my family, the arts, animals and myself. You are such a strong encourager to me and I am a blessed woman for having you as my Father. Thank you for making your family and the Lord the center of your heart. I love you.*
- *From your granddaughter —Your grasp of literature was a huge help to me in understanding the classics. I am very proud of you Papa David!*
- *From your grandson - Your passion and determination for writing have taught me to never give up on my dreams and that anything can be accomplished by simply setting your mind to it.*
- *From your grandson — I will always remember the stories you told us growing up. Your love and knowledge of literature have shone through in this work. Congratulations!*

David A. Lariscy

Table of Contents

Synopsis

A play, *Hamlet II, King of Denmark,* suggested by the last scene of William Shakespeare's *The Tragedy of Hamlet, Prince of Denmark.*

In the closing scene of Shakespeare's *Hamlet,* King Claudius, Queen Gertrude, and Laertes, son of Polonius, are dead.   Hamlet is dying, after being stabbed with a poisoned foil by Laertes. With Hamlet's death, there is no lineal heir to the Danish throne.

With his dying breath, Hamlet implores his friend, Horatio, to:

> *"Absent thee from felicity awhile,*
> *And in this harsh world draw thy breath in pain,*
> *To tell my story."*

This line suggests the plot for the play, *Hamlet II King of Denmark.* Hamlet, while a student in Wittenberg, unknowingly fathered a son by Francesca, daughter of

Hamlet II

Gonzalo, the Duke of Siena, Italy. Horatio learned this before leaving Wittenberg to attend King Hamlet's funeral and Gertrude's marriage to Claudius. When Horatio tells Hamlet that he has fathered a son who is the lineal heir to the throne. Hamlet charges Horatio with the task of placing Hamlet's son on the throne of Denmark. Hamlet names Horatio Lord Chamberlain before he dies.

Fortinbras, a Prince of Norway, bears an ancient grudge against Denmark because his father lost a war to Hamlet's father, and Norway had to cede lands and pay tribute to Denmark. However, Fortinbras had obtained permission from Claudius to allow his army to cross Denmark to wage war against Poland.

On his return from Poland, Fortinbras stops at Elsinore and finds the royal family dead. Fortinbras claims the throne based on territorial rights and the strength of his army. The nobility is forced to recognize him as king.

When Horatio tells Fortinbras that Hamlet sired a son who is rightful heir to the Danish throne, Fortinbras rejects the claim and sends Horatio to Siena, where Francesca lives with her son. The Duke, Gonzalo, is enraged when he learns that Fortinbras has rejected Hamlet's son and threatens military action against Denmark through an alliance with the Pope.

Horatio asks to join the Duke's forces and the Duke puts him in charge.

Horatio courts Francesca and with the Duke's permission asks her to marry him.

Fortinbras puts a bounty on Horatio for defecting to the Duke.

An assassin attacks Horatio, a duel ensues, and the assassin dies.

Hamlet II

Voltemand brings news that Fortinbras while hunting was fatally gored by a wild boor and died without naming an heir to the throne. The nobility wants Horatio to serve as Regent to young Hamlet.

The Duke, Horatio, Francesca and young Hamlet travel to Denmark for Horatio's investiture as Regent and his marriage to Francesca.

After the investiture scene, there is the final scene in which Horatio on the battlement of Elsinore addresses the spirit of Hamlet. After Horatio's soliloquy and exit, a voice from off the stage says:

> *O good Horatio, this is Hamlet. Now can I go to my eternal rest. My faithful friend, thou hast done well. Now the rest is indeed silence.*

King of Denmark

Hamlet II

DRAMATIS PERSONAE

Corpses of Claudius, Gertrude and Laertes
And Hamlet dying, Prince of Denmark
Horatio, Friend of Hamlet
Fortinbras, Prince of Norway
Gonzalo, Duke of Siena, Italy
Francesca,   Gonzalo's daughter
Maria, wife of Gonzalo
Young Hamlet, illegitimate son of Hamlet
Voltemand, a Courtier
Cornelius, a Courtier
Bernardo, a Watchman
Marcellus, a Watchman
Eric, a Danish Nobleman
William, a cook
Percy, cook's assistant
Assassin
Priest
Lords, Ladies, Officers, Soldiers, Messengers
and Attendants

Hamlet II

Act I, Scene I

Elsinore Throne Room
The corpses of Claudius, Gertrude and Laertes are lying about
Voltemand, Cornelius and others are standing around.
Hamlet is cradled in Horatio's arms.

Hamlet I am dying, Horatio. Tell the world that I did all that may become a man. Render a faithful account of one who could not right a wrong except through death, mine own and my villain-uncle's who murdered my father.

Horatio My dear lord, stay death a while to hear my news with which I had hoped to grace your ears when you wore Denmark's crown. Before leaving Wittenberg, Francesca, whom you courted with strong assertions of love, visited me. With tearful eyes and in quivering voice told me she had borne you a son.

Hamlet II

Hamlet

Yes, Horatio, I loved the fair Francesca, a radiant maiden, who would have been my queen had not this insidious poison prevented me.

O God! Horatio, a son!

I go to my death with most glorious news! Before the shroud of death envelops me, I entreat you, on your honor as my dearest friend, to see that my son assumes his rightful place as King of Denmark. Fortinbras, I fear, will pursue Norway's ancient claim. Let him not usurp the throne from my son.

Horatio

O, Sire, lay not that onerous burden upon me. I am too frail a vessel to sail upon such stormy seas.

Hamlet

Deny me not, Horatio. You are my only hope that my son shall one day wear Denmark's crown.

Horatio

I am not of royal blood nor do I rank among the nobility. What means have I to enforce your son's claim? I have not the power to oppose Fortinbras.

King of Denmark

Hamlet   I shall give you what power I have. The means you must find for yourself. Call Voltemand and Cornelius here quickly. I have yet a thing to say before I die.

Horatio   Ho! Voltemand and Cornelius come quickly.

Voltemand and Cornelius come and gather around Horatio and Hamlet.

Hamlet   Oh, my good friends, Voltemand and Cornelius. With the King's death, I have the power of your sovereign until my last breath. Witness that I declare Horatio Lord Chamberlain of Denmark to conduct the affairs of our state.

Voltemand and Cornelius   [*in unison*] We do so witness, noble Lord.

Hamlet   O, good Horatio, my spirit, like my father's, shall not rest until you, like the sun lighting the bleakest dawn, brightens my eternal night with news that my son sits upon the throne of Denmark.

Hamlet II

Hamlet   Tell Francesca that my love for her was my dying word.

Farewell, my friends.   This insidious potion has run its course and quite o'er-grows my spirit.   [*Dies*]

Horatio   Farewell, most noble Prince. The sad state of Denmark shall never know the loss of greatness it has suffered with your death. I shall not rest until your son is King.   [*Lays Hamlet down*]

Enter Attendant

[*Excitedly*] Sir, Fortinbras, Prince of Norway, returning from the Polish wars, begs an audience with the King.

Horatio   Bid him enter

Exit Attendant

King of Denmark

Fortinbras

Who can report on this royal carnage which offends my sight?

Horatio

I, Horatio, Lord Chamberlain, and friend to him who should have been King.

I shall assail your ears with a strange story. Of Lord Hamlet who sought to avenge his father's murder. You shall hear of Claudius, a cowardly murderer and a malevolent pretender to the throne. This and more you shall hear.

An adulterous wife who by intemperate behavior drank poisoned wine. You shall know of treacherous young Laertes who through mischance shared a fatal envenomed foil with Lord Hamlet.

I shall give you a full account of these sorry events that now leave the unhappy state of Denmark without a monarch.

Fortinbras

[*Aside*] With Hamlet's death, the throne of Denmark stands vacant. Norway has some ancient and neglected right in this fair country.

Fortune has smiled upon me. Here stand I with a victorious army and the throne of Denmark empty. I shall pluck this royal plum by right of threatened conquest. I cannot be denied.

Horatio, Hamlet's father defeated my father upon the field of battle and exacted tribute from Norway. Is it not just that I should claim the realm denied my father?

Horatio

The throne of Denmark cannot be claimed, Fortinbras. It must be granted by election of the nobility.

Fortinbras

I have twenty thousand veteran soldiers camped in your fields. I have no doubt that will warrant my election by your nobility.

King of Denmark

Horatio

[*Aside*] Shall I tell him there lives a Hamlet who is rightful heir to the throne? It is true. Denmark cannot challenge Fortinbras' armed might. The nobility will be forced to elect him to the throne. No, the time is not right. Let events unfold a while.

Fortinbras

Why so pensive, Horatio?

Horatio

I grieve for the death of my friend. By your leave may I bear the body of Lord Hamlet to a place of honor?

Fortinbras

[*taking charge*] It shall be done. Hamlet shall have a soldier's burial.

Remove the fallen.

Horatio, follow and counsel me how I shall relate this dreadful tale to the people and make known my rightful claim to Denmark's throne.

Exeunt

Hamlet II

Scene II

Throne room. Fortinbras sitting on elevated throne. Horatio, Voltemand,
Cornelius, Bernardo, Marcellus, noblemen and attendants around about.
The nobility of Denmark has elected Fortinbras King.

Throughout this scene, Fortinbras is enjoying his new kingship. He slouches
on the throne, toys with his scepter, throws Horatio questions as he walks
around the room admiring the royal furnishings.
The court waits for him to speak.

Fortinbras

Horatio, I am now your sovereign. I want you to relate to your King and this court how I came to witness so much villainy.

You say King Hamlet's ghost appeared on the battlements to charge Lord Hamlet to avenge his murder by his brother Claudius?

How came Lord Hamlet and you to be upon the ramparts like common watchmen?

Fortinbras is handed a cup of wine and puts on a skeptical smile.

Did the apparition summons you both?

Hamlet II

Court audience titters at his comment.

Horatio Yes, your majesty, in a manner of speaking it did.

Fortinbras [*very seriously*] How so?

Horatio Sire, these watchmen, Bernardo and Marcellus, came and told me an improbable tale of a ghostly presence that visited them upon the battlements during the witching hours. Permit them to speak, Sire.

Fortinbras Speak.

Bernardo By your leave, Sire. I am a soldier and have seen such ghastly sights as would appall the devil. But the ghostly vision of which Horatio speaks taught me fear I have never known.

Marcellus It is true, Sire. Bernardo speaks true. The bodiless spirit clothed in battle armor would strike terror in the bravest men.
Because Horatio is a scholar, we thought the spirit would speak to him and say why it disturbed our watch.

King of Denmark

Marcellus We implored him to join our next guard.

Fortinbras [*ignores them*] Did this apparition appear to you as well, Horatio?

Horatio It did, my Lord, though it had the bodily form of the late King Hamlet, dressed in full armor with raised visor and with a countenance more of sadness than anger, it moved like transparent mist suspended above the platform.

Fortinbras This is indeed most strange, Horatio. Say on.

Horatio Sire, the spirit made no utterance. Its insubstantial form drifted from place to place about the platform. I thought it seemed troubled, sad, and angry all at once.

Fortinbras Stayed it long?

Horatio Only minutes it seemed, Sire, but so appalled were we that only when it had faded into the night did we hear the bells toll half past the midnight hour.

Hamlet II

Fortinbras   This tale grows more astonishing with each revelation. You say this incorporeal form was like old King Hamlet?

Horatio   Yes, my Lord. Often have I seen King Hamlet in pageants, parades and other ceremonious duties. I knew him well. Bernardo and Marcellus saw the King as well.

Bernardo   Horatio speaks true, your majesty. I served King Hamlet, man and boy, thirty years. This vision was not more like.

Marcellus   Your Majesty, because the apparition was like old King Hamlet himself, we beseeched Horatio to tell Lord Hamlet forthwith.

Fortinbras   [*ignores them again*]   Why only Hamlet? A strange, unexplained vision confronts your sight. Should you not have informed the King, your sovereign, first?

King of Denmark

Horatio   Yes, Sire. One would say it was our duty to tell King Claudius of the mysterious spirit that floated above his ramparts, but in truth, my Lord, the spirit appeared in a form like that of Hamlet's departed father. We felt it presaged something touching only Lord Hamlet. Thus, did we decide to inform him first.

Fortinbras   How did Hamlet receive your news?

Horatio   My Lord, when I told him the specter appeared in form and dress like his father's, he would not let belief take hold of him.

I urged him to stand the watch with us, and if the ghost appeared, it might speak to him. That very night Lord Hamlet watched with us upon the battlement.

Fortinbras   [*Again with skepticism*]   And did Hamlet's ghostly father appear?

Horatio

Sire, long after the midnight hour passed, the air grew colder and gray mists whirled round about. Suddenly the ghost appeared in dress and form as before.

It beckoned Lord Hamlet to follow him, as if he wanted to impart something only for his Lordship's ears. I beseeched him not to follow, fearing the spirit was an evil demon luring Lord Hamlet to his destruction over the battlement wall.

Fortinbras

And did Hamlet follow?

Bernardo

Indeed, my Lord. His Lordship drew his foil and threatened to run us through if we prevented him. He then disappeared into the mists and stayed so long that we grew alarmed and prepared to follow him when he reappeared affrighted and trembling.

Fortinbras

[*ignores Bernardo*] That is little wonder. Say on, Horatio.

King of Denmark

Horatio

Sire, his Lordship would not tell us what had happened. He made us swear with an oath upon his sword that we would not tell what we had seen that night.

Lord Hamlet said if he put on a strange and unusual disposition for us not to reveal that we knew why he was acting that way.

Fortinbras

How did Hamlet proceed, Horatio?

Horatio

Your majesty, I did not know then what Lord Hamlet's ghostly father had told him on the battlements.

Lord Hamlet told me later that the spirit charged him to avenge his father's foul murder by his brother Claudius. So abhorrent was the ghost's news that Lord Hamlet thought that perhaps the devil was deceiving him to commit a heinous act.

Hamlet II

Horatio

He said the devil has power to assume a pleasing shape. Thus, he dare not commit regicide without evidence more substantial than a spectral visitation; else, the people might believe he was trying to gain the throne from which he was unjustly deprived.

So Lord Hamlet began to form a plan whereby he could be certain that the supernatural command was not calumny and he could overthrow the King with impunity.

Fortinbras

To kill a king is against God's will, Horatio.

Horatio

Is it God's will, Sire, that a man be made a king through the villainous and malicious acts of seducing his brother's wife; committing Cain's offense; and plotting the murder of his nephew? All these are offenses against heaven.

King of Denmark

Fortinbras   It is not for us to judge a king's actions; a king answers only to God. It matters not how Claudius assumed the throne. To oppose a king is a sin against the Almighty, punishable by eternal damnation.

But say on, Horatio, how did Lord Hamlet proceed in his plot to destroy his step-father and avenge his father's death?

Horatio   Not destruction, my Lord, but retribution for acts so vile they must be punished in this life — not in the hereafter.

Fortinbras   [*Testily*] You tread upon my patience, Horatio.

Horatio   Sire, Lord Hamlet had no villainous intent to kill the King. He sought a way to prove Claudius' fratricide and force his abdication.

Fortinbras   The hour grows late. Proceed with your story.

Horatio

Sire, soon after Lord Hamlet put on an antic disposition. His mother became worried that Hamlet's peculiar behavior was grief over his father's death and his mother's hasty marriage. But Polonius, the Lord Chamberlain, the King's most trusted advisor, had another reason: Hamlet was mad for the love of Ophelia, Polonius' daughter.

Horatio

Polonius suggested that they hide behind an arras in the lobby where Lord Hamlet sometimes walked in the afternoon. Polonius instructed Ophelia to encounter him there while they listened to their conversation.

Fortinbras

Was Polonius' suspicion confirmed by this deception?

Horatio

Not to the satisfaction of the King, Sire. Lord Hamlet continued his antic ways and in a rambling tirade denied his love for Ophelia. The King said though Hamlet's speech lacked form, it was not like madness.

King of Denmark

Fortinbras   What course did the King take that led to the regal massacre I witnessed upon my return from Poland?

Horatio   My Lord, the King summoned Rosencrantz and Guildenstern, Hamlet's boyhood friends, to come and spend some time with him and learn the cause of his strange behavior. Rosencrantz and Guildenstern would have had Lord Hamlet believe they came of their own volition, their only desire to visit their childhood friend, but his Lordship was not fooled.

Fortinbras   What do you mean, Horatio?

Horatio   Your Lordship, through clever questioning, Lord Hamlet elicited their confession that the King had summoned them to observe and report on his behavior.

Rosencrantz and Guildenstern also brought news that a troupe of traveling players from the city had come to perform at Elsinore.

Hamlet II

Fortinbras   I doubt the players could provide entertainment to cure Lord Hamlet's feigned melancholy or thwart his planned overthrow of the King.

Horatio   On the contrary, my Lord. The players, whom his Lordship had seen many times, provided the means by which he hoped to entrap the King and satisfy himself that it was truly his father's spirit he had seen.

Horatio   Indeed, Lord Hamlet told me, *"The play's the thing wherein I'll catch the conscience of the King."*

Fortinbras   And how did Lord Hamlet propose to catch the King's conscience? The King confesses only to God.

Horatio   Lord Hamlet asked the players to enact the *Murder of Gonzago* for the pleasure of the King and his court, but with the addition of some lines he would write.

His Lordship said he would have the players enact the scene of this father's murder—as his ghost-father had told him.

King of Denmark

Fortinbras   And how was that, Horatio?

Horatio   My Lord, while sleeping in his garden in the afternoon as was his habit, his brother Claudius stole upon him and poured hebenon in his ear!

Fortinbras   A ghastly death for a King—to die with all his imperfections on his head!

Horatio   Your Lordship, did you not counsel me that a king has no imperfections in this world?

Fortinbras   Mend your speech, Horatio, lest you imperil your life.

Horatio   Forgive me, Sire. So the stage was set, as they say. The King and his court assembled to see the play. At the point where Gonzago was poisoned, the King rose, alarmed, called for light and stormed from the court with the Queen.

Fortinbras   Did Hamlet pursue the King?

Hamlet II

Horatio

No, my Lord. Lord Hamlet was elated and said he would take the ghost's words for a thousand pounds. He was now convinced that Claudius had murdered his father. And he saw that the court had witnessed the King's reaction. Lord Hamlet said it was as good as a confession.

But he was promptly commanded to go to the Queen. She sorely reprimanded him for his conduct. Unknown to Lord Hamlet, Polonius had hidden behind the arras to listen and report to the King.

When Lord Hamlet severely berated his mother for marrying Claudius, Polonius thought the Queen was about to be harmed, so he cried out. Hamlet ran his foil into the curtain, killing old Polonius.

Fortinbras

Was Hamlet not punished for this despicable crime?

King of Denmark

Horatio

Indeed, he was, my Lord. He was immediately exiled to England, escorted by Rosencrantz and Guildenstern, where in a secret dispatch to the English monarch, the King ordered the immediate execution of Hamlet. But Lord Hamlet thwarted the King's plan by stealing the dispatch and writing a new one in which the execution of Rosencrantz and Guildenstern was ordered instead.

Fortinbras

Indeed, the English ambassadors confirmed their deaths.

But how did Lord Hamlet return to Denmark?

Horatio

Sire, Lord Hamlet's ship was attacked by pirates and during the fight, he slipped aboard the pirate's ship. He promised them a great reward if they would return him to Denmark. Lord Hamlet sent two sailors to bring me—and gold for the pirates—to join him and together we made our way back to Elsinore.

Hamlet II

Fortinbras

The King then knew that his plan to have Lord Hamlet executed had gone awry.

Horatio

Even so, my Lord. But more great tragedy awaited Lord Hamlet. Ophelia, grieving over her father's death, committed suicide.

Fortinbras

Thus, Lord Hamlet now has the blood of two on his hands–

Horatio

–and, Sire, the wrath of Laertes, Ophelia's brother, who now seeks Lord Hamlet's death. Your Lordship said the hour grows late so I shall conclude the lamentable story of Lord Hamlet's suffering.

The King saw an opportunity in Laertes' anger and suggested a fencing contest between Lord Hamlet and Laertes. Lord Hamlet accepted against my counsel.

King of Denmark

Horatio

Laertes on the King's orders envenomed the tip of his foil and during one of their exchanges, wounded Lord Hamlet. In another exchange, they swapped foils and his Lordship wounded Laertes; thus, both were poisoned; meanwhile, Claudius poisoned a cup of wine intended for Hamlet, but the Queen drinks from it. As he lay dying, Laertes confesses to Hamlet that it was all the King's treachery.

Hamlet, finally enraged beyond restraint, and unmindful of punishment in this life or the next, stabs the King, then forces some of the poisoned wine down his throat. And that, Sire, is the cause of the sorrowful scene you witnessed.

Fortinbras

Horatio, this is indeed a woeful story. Let Denmark be one general state of grief for these who have fallen. They shall be interred according to their stations and the populace shall render their mourning duties.

Exeunt

Hamlet II

Scene III

Duke Gonzalo's garden in Siena.
Francesca is alone with young Hamlet.

Francesca

[*Writing*] My Dearest Hamlet. I see you reflected in my babe's eyes. Four seasons now have passed and no word from you. You promised to return to Wittenberg and take me to wife, not knowing I carried your babe in my womb.

I do fear you are in some danger ----even your life imperiled. I pray earnestly for your welfare and implore God to shelter you and bring you safely back to me.

My father threatens to send me to a convent for the shame I have brought to his house. He says that if I have borne the son of a prince destined to be a king, such a royal personage would honor his paternity with marriage.

He has written to your uncle demanding that you come to Siena and marry me.

Hamlet II

Francesca

Oh, Hamlet, my love, what shall I do?

My impatient arms ache to embrace you.

I suffer the torment of absent love,

And I seek comfort from Heaven above.

Exit Francesca

King of Denmark

Hamlet II

Act II, Scene I

Elsinore Throne Room. Fortinbras seated on throne.
Noblemen and attendants round about.

Fortinbras   Summon Horatio, the Lord Chamberlain.

Attendants   Yes, Sire.

Enter Horatio

Horatio   Your pleasure, Sire?

Fortinbras   Horatio, your courtiers, Voltemand and Cornelius, confirmed your report that Lord Hamlet with his dying breath named you Lord Chamberlain. Out of respect for Lord Hamlet, I accept you in that office.

Horatio, do you not know why I claim the throne of Denmark?

Horatio   Why? My Lord.

Hamlet II

Fortinbras

I lost a father-king too on the field of battle by the hand of Hamlet's father. Thus, was Norway compelled to relinquish territory to Denmark.

These many years I implored my uncle-king to allow me to reclaim these lands, but he chose an uneasy peace to righteous warfare.

My uncle-king forbade me to proceed with my essay of arms against Denmark, and, instead, divert my men and arms against the Polack. My uncle-king secured from your uncle-king permission for safe conduct across Denmark to Poland.

So, either destiny or providence brought my army to Denmark's doorstep at a propitious moment when the crown is vacant. I herewith declare and embrace my sovereignty of Denmark.

I have twenty-thousand troops encamped at Elsinore to secure my right to Denmark's throne.

King of Denmark

Our mourning duties are done. Claudius, Gertrude, Laertes and Hamlet have been laid to rest with all due reverences and obsequies. Horatio, have you further news touching these sorrowful deaths?

Horatio

No, my Lord. My news touches your person.

Fortinbras

How so?

Horatio

It is true that no heirs in the Hamlet line are here on Danish soil to challenge your right to claim the throne, but there is one now living on foreign soil whose claim is superior to yours.

Fortinbras

You speak in riddles, Horatio. Say plainly what you mean.

Horatio

Your Lordship, Lord Hamlet sired a male child while at Wittenberg who is now with his mother, Francesca, in Italy. Lord Hamlet was denied the throne by Claudius' deceit; Hamlet's son should not suffer the same disgrace.

Hamlet II

Fortinbras   [*Angrily*] Horatio, you astound me
with this shocking news. I ask
you for counsel on how to bring
my claim to Denmark's crown
to the people and you say that
my claim is fraudulent. No,
worse than fraudulent—it is
baseless.

Hamlet's bastard son, though
not born on Denmark's soil and
his illegitimacy notwithstanding,
is rightful heir to this royal
jewel? Answer me, Horatio; do
the ancient laws of succession in
Denmark grant a bastard a regal
reward?

Horatio   My Lord, it is more than law.
Blood has more claim to this
crown than all the laws scribbled
upon parchment.

Fortinbras   How shall it be proved,
Horatio?

The bastard child might be
yours or any other Wittenberg
student who sought sinful
pleasure and satisfaction with
this wench called . . . what say
you? Her name?

King of Denmark

Horatio   Francesca, my Lord. And she is
of noble lineage. Her father,
Gonzalo, is the Duke of Siena, a
prosperous region in Italy. She is
beautiful and graceful, well
spoken and conversant in
several tongues. No wench she,
for from her womb has sprung
the lawful heir to Denmark's
throne.

Fortinbras   [*Haughtily*] We shall see, Horatio.
The nobility has lawfully elected
me sovereign of Denmark. I
abjure this false claim.

Horatio   Your Lordship, while tending to
court business as Lord
Chamberlain, I found this letter
to Claudius from the Duke
Gonzalo. In it, he demands that
Lord Hamlet return to Siena and
marry his daughter; furthermore,
he demands under threat of
military action that Claudius
abdicate the throne in Lord
Hamlet's favor. Both Claudius
and Lord Hamlet are beyond the
reach of Gonzalo's demand, but
what shall he say when he learns
that you have usurped the
throne while his grandson a
legitimate heir lives?

Fortinbras

[*Angrily*] Mend your speech, Horatio, or else you shall not live to see the sun rise. As for Gonzalo, I care not what he may say or do.

Horatio

Your Majesty, you have returned triumphant from the Polish wars. Poor Denmark has suffered these recent tragedies.
Do not let it be torn asunder by war.

I propose that Lord Hamlet's child be crowned King, but with your Lordship acting as Regent, governing in his name through a privy council until he reaches the age of reason, which in our country, since the memory of man runs not to the contrary, is twelve years of age.

Fortinbras

You would have your King subject himself to the humiliation of ruling through a body of old men who could question his decisions, overrule his actions and reduce him to an ineffectual figurehead? No, Horatio, Fortinbras will not be a fawning fool to your Privy Council,

King of Denmark

begging on bended knees, may I
levy this tax, kind sirs, or may I
demand our tribute from
England if you please?

No, Horatio, the King's power
is absolute, as I have reminded
you. I will not yield the throne
nor will I dilute my power by
sharing it with some old
graybeards.

As for Duke Gonzalo, we want
you to travel to his provincial
province and relate to him the
tragic events at Elsinore.
Deliver our letter in which we
shall inform him that we now
occupy Denmark's throne under
the right of territorial claims and
lawful election.

We do not acknowledge his
daughter's child as Hamlet's;
hence, there is no claim against
our crown. Inform him that any
armed threat against the
sovereignty of Denmark shall be
crushed like an eggshell. The
combined might of both
Denmark and Norway would be
too formidable for his meager
army

Hamlet II

Horatio Your Majesty, Lord Hamlet and I were students at Wittenberg. I know that he loved Francesca. He often neglected his studies to spend time with her. I have no doubt she has borne his son.

Fortinbras It matters not, Horatio. I am lawfully on the throne. The situation is the same as when Hamlet was deprived of Denmark's crown by his uncle. Regardless of how legitimate Hamlet's alleged son's claim might be, I occupy the throne and here I shall sit and rule this great country.

Now will you carry out my order or shall I find a new Lord Chamberlain?

Horatio I shall leave on the morning tide, my Lord.

Exeunt

King of Denmark

Hamlet II

Scene II

Duke's court at Siena. Duke seated on throne. Francesca, Maria, nobles, attendants round about.

Duke Call forth the messenger from Denmark.

Enter Horatio.
Francesca, recognizing Horatio, rushes to embrace him.

Francesca O, gentle Horatio, how good to see you well. Is not Lord Hamlet with you?

Horatio No, my Lady. It is my sad duty to bring tragic news to you and your father. I know no easy way to say this. Lord Hamlet is dead.

Francesca *(breaking into tears)* O horrible, most horrible! Never felt I pain till now. Hamlet's son an orphan and never looked upon by his father.

Give me your dagger, Horatio, and I will join Lord Hamlet. I shall have in death what God denied me in life!

Lunges for Horatio's dagger

Hamlet II

Horatio restrains her.
Maria comes and embraces sobbing Francesca

Maria

O my daughter. Think not of death. Live for your son's sake.

Come with me to the Holy Father who shall comfort you.

Francesca

I shall have no comfort until I know the manner of my Hamlet's death.

Tell me, Horatio, how came my Hamlet's death?

Duke

Francesca, there will be time hereafter to hear the tragic story of Hamlet's death, but leave us now.

Madam, [*motioning to his wife*] attend your daughter.

Exit Francesca crying profusely with mother comforting her.

I know you not, sir but I see you are my daughter's friend who calls you Horatio. Welcome to Siena.

King of Denmark

You have brought us sad news. Do you have other business with us?

Horatio

My name is Horatio, Lord Chamberlain of Denmark. I come from King Fortinbras with his letter in which he answers your letter to Claudius, late King of Denmark.

Horatio hands letter to the Duke who hands it to an assistant to read.

Assistant

[*reading*] To the most honorable Duke of Siena, Italy.

Greetings, May God give you peace and prosperity. We must relate most lamentable news to your Lordship.

King Claudius is dead, killed by Lord Hamlet, your daughter's supposed lover. An envenomed foil in the hands of one Laertes killed Lord Hamlet.

My emissary, Horatio, can relate the particulars of these and other deaths at Elsinore.

Hamlet II

Assistant

Now to the matter contained in your letter to the late King Claudius. Lord Hamlet's death nullifies your demand for his return, lest you have power to call him from beyond the grave.

I reject your claim that Francesca's son is an issue of Lord Hamlet's. He might be the son of any Wittenberg student, perhaps, even he who stands before you now. There is no proof he is of a royal line.

Duke interrupts reading.

Duke

[*angrily*] No proof! What slanderous words are these?

Lord Hamlet robbed my daughter of her maidenhead, seduced her with sweet sayings and pledges of eternal love. My daughter tells me a comparison of her babe to a counterfeit likeness of Lord Hamlet would confirm his paternity beyond all doubt.

King of Denmark

Horatio   My Lord, I know that Lord Hamlet loved your daughter more than life itself. He told me so many times. I have no doubt that young Hamlet is indeed Lord Hamlet's issue.

Assistant   My Lord, there is more to read.

Duke   Read on.

Assistant   [*reading*] Further, we caution you that to take warlike steps against us would bring quick and complete defeat. Doubt not that the strength of Denmark and Norway would annihilate an army of your feeble strength.

Given under my hand and seal, Fortinbras.

Duke   Horatio, you shall convey my answer to your King. Let him be aware that our feeble kingdom has allies, which let his wisdom fear.

Our border joins the Papal States. His Holiness would like nothing better than an excuse to bring the Lutheran State of Denmark into the Catholic fold.

Hamlet II

Duke

The Pope would deem it a holy war for a righteous purpose.

Tell your King to abdicate in favor of young Hamlet and you shall serve as Regent to him. Fortinbras' failure to do so is at his peril.

Horatio

Your Grace, as Lord Hamlet lay dying in my arms, I made a solemn vow to him that I would devote myself to placing his son upon the throne of Denmark.

I cannot in good conscience continue to serve Fortinbras. I pray you allow me to stay here in Siena and serve you. Together let us make preparations to restore a Hamlet and your grandson to the throne of Denmark.

Duke

Good Horatio, I accept your offer. You may reside here with us as one of our family. But Horatio, my consent has a condition: You shall lead my army to regain the throne for my grandson.

King of Denmark

Horatio   I am honored, Sire. I willingly and gladly welcome such opportunity.

Duke   My scribe shall compose the necessary dispatches to Fortinbras.

But now let us eat and drink while you, Horatio, relate the sad happenings in your former country.

I pray you, Horatio, console my daughter that she may endure this dark hour.

Horatio   Sire, I shall do all within my power to comfort Francesca as she mourns her great loss.

Exeunt

Hamlet II

King of Denmark

Hamlet II

Act III, Scene I

Elsinore Throne room.
Enter Fortinbras, Noblemen and attendants.

Fortinbras   Permit the Duke's emissary to come into our presence.

Attendant leaves stage and returns with Duke's emissary.

Emissary   Greetings from Duke Gonzalo of Siena, Italy, your Highness. I bring the Duke's response to your letter delivered to him by your Lord Chamberlain, Horatio.

Hands the letter to attendant

Fortinbras   Before we read the Duke's letter, tell me where is my Lord Chamberlain? Why is he not with you?

Emissary   Sire, I am not empowered to speak further. The letter contains all and must speak for itself.

Fortinbras   Very well.

Hamlet II

Fortinbras takes letter from attendant and begins to read.
After reading, he flings it on the floor.

Murmuring among the company.

Fortinbras

[*Angrily*] How dare the master of this little province threaten the great state of Denmark. The roguish Duke writes that if I do not surrender the throne to his bastard grandson, he will enlist the aid of the Papal States to seize our throne by force. It is an idle threat. The Popish emperor's army cannot sustain such a distant battle. He could not keep an army provisioned from Rome. Our joint forces of Denmark and Norway would push them into the sea before they gained a foothold in our land.

Does the Duke not know I am soldier? I know warfare. Have I not marched twenty thousand men across Denmark to sack Poland? The Duke's threat is as dangerous as a toothless, claw-less tiger.

But my rage increases twenty-fold by this news: Our Lord

chamberlain, Horatio, has defected and pledged his allegiance to the Duke. He will lead the Duke's army against me.

[*Angrily*] A hundred pounds to the man who first brings this traitor's head to me.

Addressing the Duke's emissary

You shall wait until my scrivener has set down my words. You may then depart in peace. Give him safe conduct.

Exeunt

Hamlet II

Scene II

Duke's palace
Horatio and the Duke are discussing Fortinbras' letter).

Duke

I cannot believe the arrogance of Fortinbras, Horatio. In harsh language, he rejects young Hamlet's claim to the throne while almost daring us to attack him. Is Fortinbras an impetuous youth with an intemperate disposition and quicksilver temper?

Horatio

Indeed, my Lord. Before old King Hamlet was murdered, Fortinbras was marshalling an army to attack Denmark to recover lands fairly won from his father by the late King Hamlet. It was only the intervention of his uncle, the King, that Fortinbras was prevented.

Hamlet II

Horatio

To assuage Fortinbras' warlike ambition, his uncle gave him permission to invade Poland to reclaim some modicum of land lost in a previous war. King Claudius gave Fortinbras permission to march his army across Denmark.

Duke

Fortinbras writes that we would encounter a two-fold defense, fighting the combined armies of Denmark and Norway. Do you think it so, Horatio?

Horatio

No, your Lordship. That is an empty threat.

Fortinbras' uncle, King of Norway, is aged and infirmed. Neither he nor his military commanders would intervene to assist Fortinbras to retain a crown spuriously won. Furthermore, with the aid of the Pope's immense armies, our forces would overwhelm the combined strength of Norway and Denmark.

My Lord, I have heard of late from Danish travelers passing through Siena from Denmark that Fortinbras reigns like a tyrant. He is over-taxing the people and persecuting his noblemen for spurious treasonous acts. I have no doubt that the nobility will support us and force Fortinbras to vacate the throne.

Duke

I shall follow your counsel, Horatio, and continue our preparations for war. My emissary is en route to Rome for an audience with the Pope. If our efforts are successful, my grandson shall be enthroned as King of Denmark before three summers have withered into fall.

Exeunt

Hamlet II

Scene III

The kitchen in Elsinore
William, the cook, and Percy, his assistant, are preparing a meal for the King.
The assistant is stirring a large pot while the cook cuts up various items for the
pot. Both of the servants are lower class and limited intelligence.

Percy   Why did the nobles make this foreigner Fortinbras our king, William?

William   Twenty thousand reasons, Percy. He has that many men at arms surrounding Elsinore.

Percy   Those be good reasons, William.

William   His soldiers who beg food from my kitchen say he is a giant as strong as ten men.

                     They say a bear mauled his guard and Fortinbras killed the beast with one blow of his powerful fist.

Percy   That be powerful, William.

William   The soldiers say his urine is so hot, it puts holes in the stones where he pisses.

Percy   That really be hot piss, William.

77

William   Ay, Percy. They say one roar of his ferocious temper could calm the Furies.

Percy   What are Furies, William?

William   They be great torrents from your mythology, Percy. But mark this, the King's personal attendant told me that once a servant spilled a cup of wine on Fortinbras and he had the poor fellow boiled alive in a tub of Rhenish.

Percy   I fear this king, William.

William   But Percy, you must serve him at his table.

Percy   William, you know I make water when I am frightened. What if I piss in my pants in his presence?

King of Denmark

Enter Attendant

Attendant   The King is hungry and calls for his food, varlets. It had better be good. The King is in a ferocious mood.

Exit Attendant

William   [*Ladling a big bowl of stew*] Take this to the King. Mind you, be careful. I shall be right behind you with the bread and wine.

Percy   [*Carefully taking the bowl of stew*] William, I be really scared.

William   Nonsense, Percy. He is just a man like you and me.

Exeunt

(The stage is bare and silent for a few minutes.)

(Suddenly, William and Percy rush onto the stage. Both visibly frightened. The front of Percy's pants is dark and he looks down and covers himself. Just as they reach center stage, Fortinbras enters with his sword drawn.)

Fortinbras   [*Loudly*] This swill is fit only for pigs! Bring me a leg of mutton or you will both boil in oil.

Exit Fortinbras

Hamlet II

William   Come, Percy. We must get a leg
of mutton cooked quickly or the
King will have our heads.

Percy   No, William. He said he would
boil us in oil.

William   Damnation, Percy! Either way
we be dead men. Come!

Exeunt

King of Denmark

Hamlet II

Act IV, Scene I

Balcony in Duke's palace
Francesca standing at railing in pensive mood
Horatio enters and Francesca turns to face him

Francesca   Oh, Horatio. How go your warlike preparations?

Horatio   Good madam, our readiness but waits upon the Pope. If he supports our efforts, I know we will be victorious.

Francesca   Horatio, I fear for your safety. Is there no way to prevent war with Denmark?

Horatio   Only if Fortinbras abdicates. There is no other way to put your son on the throne. But let us not talk of war, my gentle Francesca.

My need is to talk of you.

Francesca turns to face Horatio.

Hamlet II

Horatio   Though the memory of Lord Hamlet still burns brightly in your heart, where every beat measures your sorrow, tears of mourning will not resurrect him. You must shake off this melancholy grief and seek a new life for yourself and young Hamlet.

Francesca   Is there a new life for me, Horatio? Who would have me?

I have disgraced my family beyond redemption. I shall join the holy sisters and spend my life pretending to repent an act of love that I would most willingly commit again.

Whether you depose Fortinbras or no, my son shall be snatched from me and sent away, lest his presence be a reminder of the shame I have brought upon my father's house.

Suddenly Francesca brightens.

Tell me, Horatio. Did you not leave a fair young maiden weeping when you left Denmark?

King of Denmark

Horatio   No, Madam, I have no one. I am not noble-born nor do I have great wealth in land and possessions. The ladies of Denmark's court had no interest in Lord Hamlet's common companion.

Oh sweet lady, you ask who would have you. I would have you to love, cherish and honor.

Dear Francesca, I offer you my love and devotion. If you will have me, a simple scholar and a soldier, I will devote my life to making you happy.

Francesca   Kind Horatio, your profession of love touches me.

(Turning to leave the balcony)

Let us go out to the garden. [*Pauses*] Tell me of your fair country and your people. Would I like it there?

First, tell me of yourself, Horatio.

Hamlet II

Horatio   Francesca, my lineage is not renowned. I was born on our farm near Leipzig. I labored with my father until I was twenty.

Horatio   I was conscripted by the King for service against invaders from the south.

In a furious battle I was wounded by a spear in my side. As I lay on the ground, I saw our King thrown from his horse not far from me.

I crawled over to the King just as an enemy was about to spear him. I found a nearby sword and rammed into the enemy's chest.

Our soldiers came and removed us to a safe place. After I recovered from my wound, the King sent for me and asked what reward I desired. I replied that I sought no reward; I did only my duty. The King was insistent, so I finally said I

King of Denmark

wanted to go to the university at Wittenberg.

The King granted my wish. It was there that I met young Hamlet.
And that is how Hamlet and I became good friends and I to Denmark.

You asked about my adopted country. Denmark is a proud land of Viking history and long held traditions of independence, neutrality, and royalty.

If you would be my wife, together we could explore this great country and live in peace and harmony with its people.

Exeunt

Hamlet II

King of Denmark

Scene II

Lobby in Duke's palace.
Horatio is alone standing at a table studying a map of Denmark.
Enter assassin with dagger from stage left, shouting and running
toward Horatio's back.

Assassin   Death to the traitor, Horatio!

Horatio turns in time to ward off the blow by throwing up his arm. Horatio
grabs the assassin's dagger hand with his left hand and twists the dagger away.
As he pushes the assassin away, Horatio draws his foil.

The assassin steps back and draws his foil. There follows a lot of swordplay,
during which the assassin retrieves his dagger. Horatio draws his dagger.
During one exchange, Horatio is slightly wounded in the arm.

The assassin clumsily lunges at Horatio with his foil and Horatio parries it
easily with his. The assassin attempts to get close to use his dagger, but
Horatio is too quick. He knocks the assassin's dagger away. And in another
exchange, Horatio plunges his dagger in the assassin's stomach, mortally
wounding him.

Assassin falls.
Horatio kneels beside the assassin.

Horatio   I know you not. Why seek you
                            my life?

Assassin   [*With his dying breath*]   King
                            Fortinbras calls you traitor and
                            promised a hundred pounds for
                            your head.

Hamlet II

Horatio   Foolish man! Had you delivered my head upon a silver platter, no gold would have lined your pockets—an early grave your only reward. May God have mercy on your soul.

Assassin dies.
Enter Duke and attendant.

Duke   What ghastly sight is this?

Horatio   Fortinbras calls me traitor and seeks my death with the promise of a hundred pounds.

Duke   Your life is in danger, Horatio. I will double the guard.

Horatio   If others seek to kill me, they must be more skillful with dagger and foil than this poor fellow. I have no fear of them.

Duke   Nonetheless, I will order the guard to be more diligent lest more villains come.

Attendant, send the captain of the guard to me and remove the piece of vermin from our sight.

Exeunt

King of Denmark

Hamlet II

Scene III

Duke's courtyard. Francesca sitting, holding young Hamlet.
Enter Horatio.

Horatio

My lady, by my faith, even as a babe, young Hamlet has a royal presence. It is in the stars that he shall rule Denmark, as his father should have. How goes it with you, madam?

Francesca

O, indeed, how goes it with you, Horatio? I was horrified to hear an assassin attacked you. My heart leaped into my throat when I thought you might be hurt or killed.
[*Suddenly*], O! Horatio, you are wounded!

Horatio

I thank you, my lady, for your concern. My heart, too, leaps in joy that you might care for me.

My wound is small and will heal quickly.

Hamlet II

Francesca   O, Horatio, you have touched my heart with your kindness and sympathy while you have lived among us. You have given me strength to look beyond my grief, and see that in young Hamlet my Lord will be daily remembered.

Tell me truly, Horatio, was I but an idle amusement or did Lord Hamlet say that he really loved me?

Horatio   He did, my lady. His love for you was his last painful utterance and had not cruel fate intervened, Lord Hamlet would have returned to marry you.

Francesca   I doubt it not, Horatio.

Horatio   O sweet Francesca, I have suffered in silent agony while you grieved for Lord Hamlet. I longed to take you into my arms and comfort you with soft words and sighs of mourning for your loss.

O dear lady, royal blood does not flow in my veins, neither can I offer you a kingdom for your home, nor have I the flowery words of a courtier to express my love, but in these months I have lived within your father's house, I have admired your beauty and your grace.

I cherish the memory of the sweet sound of your voice singing lullabies to young Hamlet in the courtyard. I often neglected my business to linger and watch you strolling in the lobby in the afternoons. I long to hold your soft hands in mine, bask in the bright luster of your eyes, and profess my love for you. My lady, you have captured my heart, which I willingly surrender. May I hope that you have some affection for me?

Francesca

Sweet Horatio, are you sure your profession of love is not pity for a young mother? Is so, true love should be built on a stronger platform.

Hamlet II

Horatio   My lady, it is your beauty, your graciousness, your wit, your smile, your laughter, your kindness, your speech, it is every part of you that built my platform of love.

Horatio   Grant me only that I may court you and perhaps in time you can learn to love me as I love you.

Francesca   I have some affection for you, Horatio. Let us walk together and talk of what our future may be.

Francesca   Perhaps my heart like a newly planted flower will be nurtured with your care and patience until it reaches the full bloom of love.

Horatio   Madam, I shall be your gardener and live upon that hope.

Enter attendant.

Attendant   Forgive me, my lady. Duke Gonzalo begs Horatio's presence forthwith. A visitor comes from Denmark for him.

King of Denmark

Horatio   I know not what peaceable
                  messenger from Denmark
                  would seek me. Your ladyship, I
                  take my leave to see your father.

(Kisses Francesca's hand)

Exit Horatio and Attendant

Francesca   What a gentle man this is. O
                  little babe, can I learn to love
                  him, as I loved your father?

Exeunt

Hamlet II

Scene IV

Duke's throne room. Duke and attendants round about.

Enter Horatio.

Duke
Horatio, a countryman of yours has arrived with news touching us both, he says.

Enter Voltemand.
Horatio is excited to see someone from home. They warmly embrace.

Horatio
Voltemand, my old friend. How stands my native land?

Voltemand
A better land than when you left it, Horatio.

Horatio
(*Laughing*) What? Made better by my leaving it, old friend?

Voltemand
No, Horatio, made better by not having that which having made you leave.

Horatio
Riddle me no riddles, Voltemand. What brings you so far from home?

Hamlet II

Voltemand   To bring you and the Duke news that will cause you to rejoice I warrant.

Horatio   O, forgive me, sir.

(Turning to the Duke)

In my joy to see a countryman, I forgot my manners. This is Voltemand, an old and trusted friend.

Duke   Welcome, Voltemand, to our kingdom. What joyful news have you to bring us?

Voltemand   Sir, King Fortinbras while hunting wild boar was gored so badly that all the skills of our physicians could not save him. Fortinbras is dead.

The nobility of Denmark has sent me to tell you that the throne of Denmark awaits its true King, young Lord Hamlet. I am further empowered to say that you, Horatio, have been chosen to act as Regent until young Hamlet reaches the age of reason and can rule for himself. This and more are set forth in this missive I am instructed to place in the Duke's hands.

Hands Duke letter

Horatio

Most welcome news indeed, Voltemand. Does not Fortinbras' uncle, King of Norway, make claim to the crown?

Voltemand

There has been no news from that kingdom since Fortinbras' corpse was returned to Norway for interment.

Horatio

Sire, Providence has smiled upon us! If the old lion of Norway is content to leave Denmark alone, we have no need of armies now. Young Hamlet is acknowledged as the rightful heir to the throne of Denmark.

Duke

It is joyful news, Horatio. I think that Providence has indeed smiled upon us.

Voltemand, I know that you have much to share with Horatio about the ebb and flow of events in your homeland.

Hamlet II

Duke

Abide with us a while before returning to Denmark.

Leave us now, I pray, as I would have a private word with Horatio.

Voltemand

Sire, I thank you for your hospitality and I embrace the opportunity to reside in your fair land.

Voltemand exits

Duke

Horatio, I doubt that my daughter will think Providence has smiled upon us. Must her son be taken from her to be raised by nurses in a foreign land?

Horatio

My Lord, your question touches both my heart and mind. In the time I have been in your service, I have come to love your daughter. When you summoned me, I was even then in the garden pledging my love to her.

King of Denmark

Duke　　　　　　　What says my daughter?

Horatio　　　　　　She says she has affection for me that with patient nurturing may blossom into love.

Duke　　　　　　　Horatio, in the time you have spent with us, I have come to look upon you as the son I never had. I have prayed that you and Francesca would come to love one another.

　　　　　　　　　　You have my permission to ask her hand in marriage. Go to her, Horatio, and share this God-sent news that her son will be King and ask her whether she desires to be the wife of Denmark's Regent.

Exeunt

Hamlet II

Scene V

Duke's courtyard.
Francesca sitting alone without young Hamlet.
Enter Horatio.
He goes to her and kneeling at her feet takes her hands in his.

Horatio Francesca, the visitor from my country was my old friend, Voltemand. He brings great news. The tyrant Fortinbras is dead. The nobility clamors for the restoration of the throne to young Hamlet.

Francesca *(naively)* Horatio, my son is but three years upon this earth and a child cannot rule a kingdom.

Horatio *(Smiling)* True, my lady. The nobility chooses me as Regent to act in young Hamlet's stead until he is twelve years old when he shall be crowned.

Francesca And what of me, Horatio? Shall I lose a son and languish here in Sienna while he gains a kingdom?

Hamlet II

Horatio   Francesca, it is my earnest desire
                       and Heaven's wish that young
                       Hamlet's mother travel to
                       Denmark to become the wife of
                       his Regent.

Francesca   *(joshingly)* If that is a proposal,
                       Horatio, it is a very subtle one.

Horatio   I am sorry, my lady. I have not
                       the eloquence to speak with
                       lover's words. But if you will be
                       my wife, I shall demonstrate my
                       love and devotion in a thousand
                       different ways.

                       Your father has given me
                       permission to seek you as my
                       wife. You said that you must
                       have time in which to learn to
                       love me.

                       Your father has also proposed a
                       way for you to earn that needed
                       time.

Francesca   What does my father want me to
                       do, Horatio?

Horatio   It is the Duke's desire that he
                       travel with us to Denmark for
                       my investiture as Regent. If
                       during our journey you can learn

to love me enough to be my wife, then Denmark will enjoy a double blessing, the restoration of a Hamlet to the throne of Denmark and the wedding of young Hamlet's Regent.

If in that time the spark of your love for me is not ignited into a flame of devotion, I shall with patience suffer the pangs of refused love and trouble you no more.

Francesca

Horatio, while you have dwelled in our midst, I have observed your gentle manner, your reticence in my presence and often wondered if you thought me plain and undesirable.

Horatio

Dear Francesca, perish the thought that I would ever think you undesirable.

Francesca

I noted too your devotion to young Hamlet and thought in my idle moments that you would make a suitable second father to him.

Francesca   If my son is to be a youthful king, he will need a father's counsel and his mother's love to guide him in the affairs of state. So I shall be your wife in Denmark!

Horatio   O, my dear lady, I shall devote every moment to bringing you such peace and happiness that the angels themselves shall be envious.

They embrace.

Exeunt

King of Denmark

Hamlet II

Act V, Scene I

Elsinore
The principal noblemen of Denmark are gathered around, awaiting the arrival
of Gonzalo, Maria, Horatio, Francesca, Voltemand and young Hamlet.
Spokesman for the nobility is Lord Eric.

Enter Duke, Maria, Horatio, Francesca, Voltemand and young Hamlet.

Eric   Welcome most honorable Gonzalo.

Welcome home, Horatio, upon this happy occasion.

Good Voltemand, you have done well.

Lady Francesca, welcome to Denmark. May you find joy and happiness here with us in Denmark.

And this is young Hamlet, our future king. He is a stout young man and much favors his noble father.

Welcome, all upon this glad time.

Duke

To one and all we greet you in the name of your future King.

Most noble Lords, my daughter, my grandson and I come to your fair land with grateful hearts. The news that young Hamlet is recognized as the rightful monarch to govern your great country pleases this ancient ear. But let me announce another happy blessing for me.

Valiant Horatio who confronted Fortinbras, challenged his claim to the Danish throne, and thwarted an assassin's dagger, has lived these three years in my dukedom. He has served me loyally. In that time he became the son I prayed for but which God never blessed me.

Now I say joy abounds within my heart to announce that I have given my daughter, Francesca, to become Horatio's wife.

Court audience murmurs and some handclapping

King of Denmark

Horatio

It is true, Lord Eric. The lovely Francesca has consented to be my wife. All of Denmark shall rejoice as God joins us in holy matrimony. Within a fortnight of my investiture, our wedding shall be performed with all attendant solemn rites.

Sire, the journey was long and arduous. Knowing that my beloved country lives in peace and harmony made the time short for me.

But for the noble Gonzalo and his family, the travel was tiring. I beg of you all, give them leave to retire. They are in much need of rest.

Eric

Most assuredly, Horatio.

Enter attendant

Attendant, escort the Duke and his family to their apartments.

Exit the Duke, Maria, Francesca and young Hamlet with attendant.

Hamlet II

Eric

Now, Horatio, we have much happy business to discuss. Arrangements are being made for your installation as Regent within a fortnight.

The ceremony will be here in the court; all the nobility of Denmark will be present. The most high bishop will conduct your installation.

After the death of tyrannical Fortinbras, we, the Earls and Dukes, some fifteen in number, convened ourselves as a body politic to govern our fair state until a successor could be selected. Expecting some repercussion from old Norway, we acted quickly to declare you as Regent in absentia for young Hamlet and dispatched Voltemand to get you and young Hamlet.

Horatio

Has there been any news from Norway?

Eric

No, the delegation that accompanied Fortinbras' body was icily received in old Norway's court. The King himself is so infirmed that he did not make an appearance. We have no knowledge whether Norway will pursue a claim to the crown based upon Fortinbras' brief reign as our sovereign.

Horatio

It is doubtful that we will be threatened from the North. With the combined strength of the Duke's army and ours, Norway would be ill advised to challenge us. Nevertheless, I have in mind a plan to pacify Norway in a peaceful way.

Eric

Which brings us to an important point, Horatio. You are not of royal blood. As you know, all of Denmark's kings have descended from a common line—until Fortinbras–although not always the eldest son. The election has fallen to you as who could lead our great state as a warrior, a statesman and a governor.

Hamlet II

Eric

The accession of young Hamlet will restore the blood line of succession, but until then you shall reign as Regent—with one proviso: we nobles will act as Privy Council to oversee your actions to insure that you do not act to the detriment of our country. Can you accept that condition, Horatio?

Horatio

I embrace your condition heartily. I would have made the same proposal, my Lord. Did you not know that I suggested to Fortinbras that he act as Regent for young Hamlet before I left for Italy and he refused?

Eric

We know Fortinbras' ambition would not let him serve in a subservient role. We are glad, Horatio, that we may crown you Regent upon this stated proscription: You shall take no action affecting the welfare of our country, undertake no foreign expeditions or interventions and levy no taxes upon the people without the prior consent of the Council.

King of Denmark

Horatio   May God give me wisdom to govern upon those conditions.

Eric   Now, Horatio, tell us of your plan to neutralize old Norway.

Horatio   Your Lordship knows young Fortinbras had ambition to reclaim certain lands forfeited by his father to King Hamlet but old Norway prohibited him; thus, Fortinbras undertook his expedition to Poland from whence he came here to seize the crown.

Eric   A regrettable episode in our history, Horatio, but what of your plan.

Horatio   The lands forfeited by old Fortinbras, except those cultivated by our peasants, are rocky, barren outcroppings, the loss of which would be of no consequence to us. I propose in the cause of peace and harmony between our countries that we offer to return these uninhabited lands in exchange for their relinquishing all claims to the Danish throne.

Hamlet II

Horatio

In this way, we extend the olive branch to old Norway without dishonoring ourselves.

Eric

I like it well. We shall define those lands to be returned and dispatch our offer to Norway. Perhaps we will also cancel the annual tribute exacted by old King Hamlet.

Eric

This day is well ended. Let us feast and make merry on this glorious day.

Exeunt

King of Denmark

Hamlet II

King of Denmark

Scene II

Elsinore throne room. The throne is vacant.
A priest is standing before the throne, facing the audience.
Gonzalo, his family, Lords, ladies and attendants round about. Music.

Horatio enters to ceremonial music and it fades as he kneels before the priest.

Priest makes the sign of the cross over the kneeling Horatio.

Priest   In thy presence almighty and merciful God, we assemble to crown thy servant, Horatio, Regent for Hamlet the Second. Under thy divine guidance grant him the wisdom to diligently and faithfully perform all duties and ceremonies befitting a monarch. Amen.

Assembled Company echoes amen.
Attendant hands the priest a coronet.
Priest holds coronet over Horatio's head as he prays.

Almighty God, who hast given us this good land for our heritage; We humbly beseech thee that we may always prove ourselves a people mindful of thy favor and glad to do thy will. Bless our land with honorable industry, sound learning and pure manners.

Hamlet II

Priest   Save us from violence, discord
and confusion; from pride and
arrogance, and from every evil
way. Endue with the spirit of
wisdom this authority of
government, that there may be
justice and peace at home, and
that through obedience to thy
law, we may show forth thy
praise among the nations of the
earth. Amen.

(Placing crown on Horatio)

Most merciful God may this
crown be a symbol of thy
approval of thy servant, Horatio,
that with thy guidance he may
govern with wisdom, dispense
justice fairly and do all things
meet and right for your people.
Amen.

Assembled Company echoes amen.

Horatio rises and advances to the throne and turns to face the audience.

Horatio   Holy Father, Lords, Ladies and
friends of Denmark, in a spirit
of humility and with God's help,
I shall faithfully execute the
office of Regent until in the
wisdom of the Privy Council

King of Denmark

Lord Hamlet shall himself be crowned your King.

It is just and right that the name of Hamlet shall again rule our great land. I am but a poor vessel in which to carry a King's burden, but I shall do all within my power to earn the honor you have given me.

Young Hamlet's father, Lord Hamlet, would have been your King had not his villainous uncle stopped his breath through vile and deceitful means. And though I am now young Hamlet's step father, I shall serve him as loyally and devotedly as I served his father.

Now I declare this a day of feasting and celebration.

Let there be music, dancing; food and drink for all,

For great Denmark rises again, nevermore to fall.

Exeunt

Hamlet II

Scene III

The battlement at Elsinore at night.
Enter Horatio alone. Horatio gazing out into the misty darkness.

Horatio

My Lord Hamlet, I stand upon the very battlement where you met the spirit of your departed father and learned of your Uncle Claudius' villainy.

O my beloved friend, could you but know the happy end of the sad business begun by your uncle-king? The tyrannical Fortinbras, backed by twenty thousand men at arms, claimed the throne in your stead. While hunting, Fortinbras stalked a wild boar alone and was killed for his mistake.

The nobility summoned your son and me from Italy, where I had resided to help the Duke of Siena raise an army and reclaim the crown in your son's name.

Hamlet II

Horatio

Your son will be crowned King as you commanded me with your dying breath, and I am blessed with a heaven-sent marriage to the beautiful Francesca. The nobles have named me Regent for your son and he will be crowned King upon his twelfth birthday.

Your Lordship would be proud of your son. He has not reached his sixth birthday and already his kingly deportment is evident. He shows an inquisitive mind and native intelligence that was his father's legacy. Young Hamlet is a handsome child with clear blue eyes the color of sky on a Spring morning, and strong features that presage resoluteness and wisdom, but tempered with a kind of gentleness that is the gift of his mother. Already he shows an eager inquisitiveness for the sporting pursuits of riding, falconry and archery. Young Hamlet has a keen wit and impish disposition. Voltemand, my Lord Chamberlain, is often the target of his pranks that send the court into raucous

King of Denmark

laughter. He will make a goodly King.

Lord Hamlet, I know you reside in that distant land from which no traveler returns, but if my words reach you, I pray you have no enmity toward me for taking Francesca for my wife. She is my dearest treasure and adorns my life as the richest jewel decorates the crown of a King.

And so my friend, for you are my dearest friend in this life and the next, I have accomplished the task you set before me. I fervently hope that your perturbed spirit can at last rest with the certain knowledge that your beloved Denmark has a bright and glorious future now that Hamlet the Second will sit upon the throne.

Hamlet II

*As Horatio is speaking, a faint vertical light begins to appear
in the corner of the stage. Horatio does not notice.
As he exits, the light becomes brighter.
Voice from off the vacant stage speaks.*

Hamlet
O good Horatio, this is Hamlet the Dane. Now can I go to my eternal rest. My faithful friend, thou hast done well. And now the rest is indeed silence.

Curtain

King of Denmark

.

Hamlet II

About the Author

David Lariscy has been a fan of the writings of William Shakespeare since childhood. His passion for

reading and writing has been heavily influenced by the Bard. After years of study and teaching in community Shakespeare groups, David has finally made a unique contribution of his own to the genre.

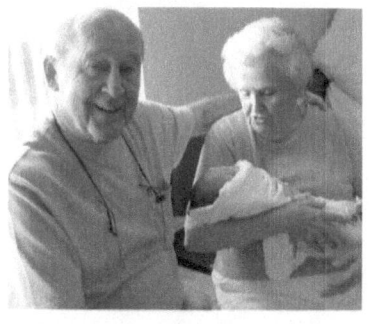

Hamlet II, King of Denmark is a compelling sequel to Hamlet that completes the story. His hope is that you enjoy this sequel almost as much as the original.

Eximius Books

www.EximiusBooks.com

Eximius is the Latin word for "Excellent," "Super," or "Exceptional." Eximius Books is dedicated to producing unique, innovative, and compelling books in the Literature and Fiction genre. If you have a work that you would like to publish, please submit a query letter via our website.

Eximius Books is an imprint of WordTruth Press℠ based in the United States.